CLAIRE WHEELER

THE ENTREPRENEURIAL HANDBOOK

Start-Up and Business Skills
for Students

THE ENTREPRENEURIAL
HANDBOOK

Start-Up and Business Skills
for Students

CLAIRE WHEELER

Published in 2024 by Amba Press, Melbourne, Australia
www.ambapress.com.au

© Claire Wheeler 2024

All rights reserved. No part of this book may be reproduced or transmitted in any form or by any means, electronic or mechanical, including photocopying, recording or by any information storage and retrieval system, without prior permission in writing from the publisher.

Cover design: Tess McCabe
Internal design: Amba Press
Editor: Rica Dearman

ISBN: 9781923116412 (pbk)
ISBN: 9781923116429 (ebk)

A catalogue record for this book is available from the National Library of Australia.

Disclaimer: The material in this publication is in the nature of general comment only, and neither purports nor intends to be advice. Readers should not act on the basis of any matter in this publication without considering (and, if appropriate, taking) professional advice with due regard to their own particular circumstances. The author and publisher disclaim all and any liability to any person, whether a purchaser of this publication or not, in respect to anything and the consequences of anything done or omitted to be done by any such person in reliance, whether whole or partial, upon the whole or any part of the contents of this publication.

Contents

Nice to meet you! — 1

Chapter 1 Introduction — 3

Chapter 2 Myth-busting — 11

Chapter 3 Step one – Discover your big idea — 19

Chapter 4 Step two – Research and test — 27

Chapter 5 Step three – Establish a business plan — 37

Chapter 6 Step four – Advertise your business — 57

Chapter 7 Step five – Money, money, money! — 73

Chapter 8 Business ideas — 89

Chapter 9 Final message — 93

Nice to meet you!

Hi, I'm Claire, and I'm super excited you're reading this book. It means you're interested in starting your own business, which is a fantastic thing to do – it might just transform your whole life!

It's safe to say I was bitten by the entrepreneurial bug at a very young age, and when I say 'bug', I mean a totally insatiable entrepreneurial superbug. In primary school, I washed cars and sold flowers in my neighbourhood. In high school, I copied music CDs and sold them on the street. I had many kid start-ups: selling homemade jewellery and cakes, cleaning houses, telling fortunes (that's a story for another time), babysitting and tutoring.

After university, I entered the world of big business and have spent more than 20 years working with some of the world's largest brands. In 2020, I set up a business selling eco-friendly cardboard desks and play spaces. My own kids participated in starting this business, and I saw how excited they were by the whole process. This was the driving force behind my next venture, setting up an entrepreneurial academy for children: Kid Biz Academy. I have now trained kids of all ages to set up their own businesses. My passion is igniting a spark in young people and helping them develop entrepreneurial skills. I want to bring my passion for entrepreneurship to children all over the world, so I wrote this book to help them see how much they can achieve when they start a business doing what they love. I hope you enjoy the read and that it inspires you to start a business of your own.

CHAPTER 1

Introduction

Being an entrepreneur and starting your own business is one of the most amazing things you can do. It's about inspiring others, learning new skills, exploring your strengths and overcoming failures. And – believe it or not – there is no age limit to success. In fact, kids as young as five years old have launched businesses and become extremely successful! There are loads of kids starting successful businesses all over the world. This book will give YOU the tools to start your own biz based on your passions.

Entrepreneur

'On – Truh – Pruh – Nuh'

What exactly is an entrepreneur? Well, it's really a fancy word for someone who starts their own business. Pretty much every single mega-successful person you've ever heard of (like, private jets and holidays to outer space success) made their money from starting a business. I'm talking the Bill Gates, Elon Musk and the Mark Zuckerbergs of this world. But it's not just about making money; there are heaps of benefits to being a business owner – more on this later.

TOTALLY AWESOME AND INSPIRING ENTREPRENEURS

Janine Allis – Boost Juice

In 2000, Janine launched her first Boost Juice store in Adelaide, South Australia. The brand rapidly grew and now boasts 550 locations in more than 13 countries worldwide. How's that for a business boost?! Janine has inspired other entrepreneurs on the TV show *Shark Tank* and is one of the most influential (and down-to-earth) Australian entrepreneurs.

Jeff Bezos – Amazon

Jeff Bezos is one of the richest people in the world and arguably one of the most well-known entrepreneurs. In 1994, he opened his own virtual bookstore while working out of his garage. 'Amazon' sold its first book in 1995 and quickly expanded to eventually become the world's largest online retailer. Not bad for a little garage bookstore, hey?

Jason Derulo – Rocket Carwash

Jason Derulo might be better known for his music career, but the singer is also a savvy entrepreneur. With 13 businesses under his belt, Jason's most successful venture is a car wash. Offering a subscription service and revolutionising the car-wash industry, the business is now valued at a cool US$2bn!*

Source: Jason Derulo

Nick Molnar – Afterpay

Selling jewellery on Ebay, Nick quickly became the highest-selling jewellery retailer on the platform. What an achievement! If that wasn't enough, Nick decided to launch Afterpay in 2015 and became one of Australia's youngest-ever self-made BILLIONAIRES.

Melanie Perkins – Canva

Melanie came up with the idea for a simple design template platform after finding traditional ones difficult to use. Today, Canva has over a hundred million monthly users and is worth – you might want to sit down for this – more than $25 BILLION!* Melanie and her co-founder received more than a hundred rejections from investors when they first started pitching their idea; the moral is that if you believe in something, don't give up!

Source: Financial Review

Failing fabulously

You're probably asking, "If being an entrepreneur gets you so stinking rich, why doesn't everyone start a business?" Well, there are a couple of reasons. First, you need to be passionate enough about something to turn it into a business. Being an entrepreneur is hard work and some people simply don't want to put in the hard yards. Also, you take a lot of risks when setting up a business – you can lose money and time, and you can fail. But I'm going to let you in on a secret. Every entrepreneur who has made it big in business has failed at something. EVERY SINGLE ONE.

Here's the thing: the failures, rejections and mistakes along the way are experiences that you need in order to learn. Every mistake we make teaches us a lesson for the future. By starting a business now, while you're still young, you can make those mistakes and figure out what works. By the time you're an adult, you'll have mastered so many business skills. Meanwhile, your mates will still be trying to catch up. Strong entrepreneurs have a fantastic work ethic. It's about getting past the failures and not giving up. That's key. You don't *win* or *lose* in entrepreneurship, as Nelson Mandela said, "You win, or you *learn*."

FAMOUS BUSINESS FAILURES

James Dyson
James Dyson, who invented the Dyson vacuum cleaner, created 5,126 failed prototypes before he landed his first working model.

Michael Jordan
The famed greatest basketball player of all time, was dropped from his high school team!

Colonel Harland Sanders
It seems incredible to believe that the founder of KFC was rejected more than a thousand times before finding a franchise partner!

Making the big bucks

Does everyone who starts a business become super rich? You *can* get super rich, but with your first business, you probably won't make any money. This isn't a bad thing, honestly, because the reason you're doing this now is to *learn*. You'll gain many skills for the future. That is the most important thing to recognise. Being an entrepreneur is about so much more than money. Don't worry, earning money will happen once you start to work things out.

Reasons to start your own biz

Why become an entrepreneur if you're not guaranteed to make heaps of money? There are so many reasons to start your own business; here are a few:

1. You get to do what you love.
2. You can choose who you work with.
3. You can choose when and where you want to work.
4. You can create a positive impact.
5. You get to fulfil your purpose.
6. You can be your own boss.
7. There's unlimited income potential.

Super skills

Starting your own business gives you the opportunity to develop top-notch skills that help later in life, regardless of whether you end up running your own company or not. It allows you to develop a growth mindset and gain personal and professional skills that will enable you to thrive in whatever you do.

AWESOME SKILLS YOU DEVELOP WHILE SETTING UP YOUR BUSINESS

Productivity skills (these are stellar skills to improve how you work):

- Planning and goal setting
- Software and application skills
- Accounting and money skills

Personal skills (these are the characteristics unique to you – your brilliant inner qualities):

- Time management
- Organisation
- Creativity
- Motivation
- Focus
- Purpose
- Empathy
- Strong work ethic

Professional skills (these skills help you shine in your work and, ultimately, succeed):

- Leadership
- Management
- Outsourcing
- Team building
- Marketing (telling people about your biz)
- Presenting your ideas
- Improving the way things are done

Mindset skills (these refer to your attitude and approach in life, and in your business):

- Learning from mistakes
- Problem solving
- Resilience (being able to bounce back from setbacks)
- Sacrifice
- Patience
- Persistence

School of life

Don't they teach this in school? In some ways, the school playground teaches more entrepreneurial skills than the classroom. Those Pokémon cards you were swapping in primary school? That was teaching you about supply and demand and peer-to-peer trading, which are essential for setting up your business. Making new friends and discovering their interests? That's teaching you about networking and relationship building. The schoolyard is also where you're encouraged to think for yourself without a teacher to guide you. This leads to some out-of-the-box thinking and creativity, which are 100% entrepreneurial skills.

Schools may not teach entrepreneurship as a core subject. They do, however, give some amazing groundwork for setting up a business, such as financial literacy (the ability to manage and understand money). But schools also don't encourage failure and, as we know, failure helps us learn, and teaches us to never give up.

In the entrepreneurial world, you would hire someone to do the tasks you didn't have the skills or time to do. That way, you could focus on other parts of the business. But if you hired someone to do your homework, you'd be sent to detention! So, you can see how these skills aren't learned in school.

This book will take you on a journey through setting up your own business. It will be your go-to manual giving you all the tools you need to become the next big thing!

Quick chapter recap

1. An entrepreneur is **someone who starts a business.**

2. You can start a business and **be a boss as young as five years old!**

3. The business you start should be based on **something you're passionate about.**

4. There are **heaps of skills you'll learn** by starting your own business (and most of these you won't learn at school).

5. This is about **more than making money.** Your first business might not make any money, but the lessons you learn will help you earn later.

6. Making mistakes is great! **Failure is part of your success.**

CHAPTER 2

Myth-busting

Let's get straight into it and smash some myths about young people in business.

Myth #1: Only grown-ups can start a business.

False! There are thousands of youngsters, just like you, who have created their own businesses. These entrepreneurs are making their money in very different ways. Check out some of their stories...

Tex Stoll – Eco Green Co

Trying to buy his mum a new phone case, 12-year-old Tex was left feeling disappointed with the plastic choices available. While researching what eco-friendly options were out there (hardly anything), he quickly saw a *gap in the market* and decided to create a biodegradable phone case, launching his business, Eco Green Co. By using sustainable materials and customising his products, Tex has created a unique brand that is truly making a difference.

GAP IN THE MARKET

A gap in the market is an opportunity to offer a product or service customers want that businesses aren't currently providing.

Indiana Robinson – Bubble Pup Salon

When Indiana's mum offered to get a dog if she agreed to groom it, Indiana jumped at the chance. She dedicated all of her time to learning how to wash, brush, de-shed and groom Daisy, as well as checking for signs of infection, nail trimming and brushing her teeth. At the age of 15, Indiana used her skills to open her business, Bubble Pup Salon, now a thriving hub for pups from all over her community.

Leah Chalhoub – Lil Leah's Candy

Leah created Lil Leah's Candy, a fun and unique candy box business, at just eight years old. How rad is that? She now offers a wide range of products, including chocolate boxes, slime candy, USA and movie treats, all beautifully displayed in Leah's fabulous DropBox packaging. Her product is even patent pending, proving that no dream is too big!

Kiana Mei – Kiana Mei Designs

After studying in Japan, 15-year-old Kiana was inspired to pursue origami. She practised the craft daily, framed her artworks and sought feedback from family and friends. Kiana then launched her own business, both online and at market stalls. Today, she successfully manages a six-figure business and hosts events to inspire and support fellow young entrepreneurs.

Getting a business partner

By teaming up with a parent or caregiver when you start your business, you can be sure all business tasks can be accomplished, even if age restrictions apply. They will be a silent partner in the business, while YOU are the boss!

Myth #2: You need a lot of money to start a business.

This is a huge myth. In fact, there has never been a better time to start a business than right now. That's because there are so many businesses you can set up for free. That's right – they have zero start-up costs. They'll cost you nothing. Nada. Zilch. Zip. OK, you get it!

From dog walking to blogging to printing T-shirts on demand, there are loads of businesses you can set up with no upfront costs.

Funding to start

In this book, you'll find start-up ideas that have minimal set-up fees. If you do require some initial investment, here are five easy ways to get it:

1. **Save your loose change.**

    Stash it away. Don't even *think* about touching it!

2. **Do odd jobs around the house or neighbourhood.**

    Make sure you remember to agree on the service and price upfront to avoid an awkward moment.

3. **Ask for money as a holiday or birthday gift.**

    And then make sure you save it. This will totally be worth it in the end!

4. **Sell something you no longer want.**

    Just make sure it's yours to begin with and you have permission to sell. Don't go selling your mum's favourite boots or your brother's video games!

5. **Borrow money from a family member.**

    Remember you will have to pay the money back, so only do this if no other option is available.

Myth #3: You don't think you have any good business ideas.

It can sometimes feel like a total brain overload trying to work out where to start. That's why you'll work through the activities in this book to come up with an idea that suits you. This book will help you generate tons of ideas, so you can be sure you'll end up doing something you love. Starting is half the battle!

Myth #4: You don't have enough time to start a business.

Between school, friends, homework, sport and other activities, it might seem like you have no spare time to set up a business. Being your own boss will definitely take time and hard work, and you may have to make some sacrifices, but it will be worth it in the end. There are always ways to manage your time more efficiently, learn how to prioritise the right tasks and build a business that will work with your life.

Tips to help manage your time:

1. **Set manageable daily tasks.**

    The key word here is 'manageable'. If you can only manage to do one thing, then make that your goal and tick it off the list. If you set unrealistic targets for yourself, you'll never achieve your goals and soon lose motivation. Setting your daily tasks can be as simple as a handwritten to-do list or an electronic diary or schedule. Keep this seriously simple. Here's an example:

	MON	TUES	WED	THURS	FRI	SAT	SUN
3:00 PM							
3:30 PM	Designing		Print Flyers		Deliver		
4:00 PM	Flyers	Finish			Flyers		
4:30 PM		Flyers					
5:00 PM							
5:30 PM							
6:00 PM							

2. **Create a calendar overview.**

   You'll use this as a basic roadmap to track where you want your business to be over the next three months, six months, one year and so on to help you stick to your goals. It's great to have this up on your wall, next to where you do most of your work.

3. **Disconnect.**

   Turn off your video games, TV, phone and other distractions so you can be more productive. If you need to, put everything on airplane mode for your scheduled work time.

4. **Schedule time in your calendar for breaks and play.**

   It's just as important to rest, relax and play as it is to work hard. These work breaks are often where inspiration strikes. Even talking to your mates can give you great ideas!

Myth #5: There are too many legal issues with starting a business.

You probably won't have thought too much about this and that's OK. It really doesn't have to be difficult. All the tax and legal info can be handled by your adult business partner (your parent or caregiver) with your input.

At some stage, when the business starts to take off, you will need to decide on a business structure. For simplicity, it is probably easiest to set up as a Sole Trader.

Depending on your business type and location, you may need a business licence*, so check out your local council and government websites for more details. Depending on your age, some states will have different regulations. Once set up, your adult partner can have the business in their name and pay you the profits as an allowance. Check what works best for you.

Tax implications may also occur, so ensure you and your partner check your local government websites.

*This is not legal advice specific to you. It is recommended to take professional legal advice from a business attorney for your project when required.

WHAT IS TAX?

When people work and earn money, the government collects a portion of that money as tax. Tax money is then used to help pay for things like roads, schools, hospitals, libraries, police and other services. The more money you earn, the more income tax you pay.

Another thing to keep in mind is that the minimum age for most social networks is currently set at 13 years old, though some networks will give a minimum age of 16 or over. It's understandable to want to have your own social pages for your business, but please respect your parents' wishes and all national and state laws. I'd recommend your business partner looks after the social pages and messaging, while you design the content for them to post.

Myth #5: You don't think you have the right skills to start a business.

You might think you don't have the right skills, but you do have one advantage over most business owners: you're very young! You have a leg up on most adults starting a business because:

- **You're a natural tech expert.** You were born and have been evolving with the internet and technology since day dot.

- **You have wicked creativity skills.** Those games you made up in the playground, the pictures you draw and the stories you tell are proof you're in tune with your imagination. You can dream up anything!

- **You're super curious.** You can see things and solve problems that most adults can't. (Solving problems is what we do as entrepreneurs, so this is an ultra-important skill. More on that later.)

- **You learn extraordinarily fast.** Children have a lot more neurons (information messengers in the brain) than adults, creating new brain connections. This means it's a scientific fact that young people can learn and memorise things better and faster than adults. How cool is that?

- **You probably already have a skill you don't realise is valuable.** Do you know how to play a musical instrument? Do you play sports or video games? Do you dance? Do you know how to sew, write, act, garden, take photographs? The list is endless!

- **It's OK for you to fail.** You're learning, so mistakes are EXPECTED. You don't have the same fear of failure as many adults do.

Live the DREAM!

Just remember, setting up a business doesn't have to be overly complicated. The next five chapters contain my five-step process for you to follow in more detail, but here is the basic concept – the DREAM formula:

Discover your big idea

Research and test

Establish a business plan

Advertise your business

Money, money, money!

DREAM BIG.

Quick chapter recap

1. **Young people can absolutely start their own business!**

2. You can **start a business for free**, or very little cost.

3. **This book will help you** find your business idea.

4. With organisation, you will be able to **find time to create a business.**

5. Your grown-up partner can **check the tax and legal information** for you.

6. **Young people already have the right skills** to start a business.

CHAPTER 3

Step one – Discover your big idea

In this first step you'll learn about the two different types of business you can start. One that sells a *product*, or one that offers a *service*.

Product vs service

A product is a physical item you sell. You could make, create or even buy something to sell. I've seen some cool product-based kids' businesses such as resin jewellery, photographic calendars, selling chicken eggs and, of course, the trusty lemonade stand.

A service is something you do for someone – offering your time and expertise to make their life better. Service-based businesses might include mowing lawns, babysitting, dog walking or even fitness classes. What you choose to do will ultimately depend on what you like and what you're good at.

PRODUCT BUSINESSES

Here are a few ideas of things to sell to tickle your imagination: keychains, slime, hand-painted rocks, homemade candles, cupcakes, dog biscuits, homemade playdough, lip balm, bath bombs, pet portrait paintings, printed T-shirts and dreamcatchers.

SERVICE BUSINESSES

Check out these services to kickstart your thinking: party planning, house cleaning, language lessons, website building, craft workshops, pet-sitting, running errands, toy repairing, sewing, custom sneaker painting, pet photography and tutoring.

Loving what you do

You'll need to work out whether you are going to start a product- or service-based business, and the first step to working this out and creating your own business is deciding what you're passionate about. The only way you'll stick to a business is if you love what you're doing. You're probably thinking, *Well, duh, that's common sense*, right? But there are still a lot of adults who don't truly get this. You see, some people start a business simply because they think it will make them lots of money, even if they don't like the work – but this way of thinking is totally wrong. Imagine setting up a cat-grooming business when you're super allergic to cats. Well, I'd guarantee that business would fail, because you'd do anything to avoid working!

That's why it's crucial to align your business with your interests. You already have your own passions, so let's identify them. It might be useful to have a think about what your interests, strengths or skills are and write them down. It can be as simple as *I'm passionate about sustainability* or *I love dogs*. Just write down your passions.

Problem solver

Another way to develop a business idea is to identify problems you or other people have and think about how you could solve them.

We saw some fantastic examples of this in the first chapter with the entrepreneurs who created Afterpay and Canva. They identified a problem and developed a business to solve that problem for their customers. We'll delve into this more as we go through the book. **All successful businesses solve problems** and if we nail this part, we'll be well on the way to making it big time!

Still clueless?

Don't panic if you can't think of your passions just yet. Not everyone is so sure of their passions or skills.

Have a go at the flowchart below to see what category you fall into. I've split Chapter 8 into the four categories you see at the bottom of the chart with business ideas for each category. If you're struggling to think of ideas right now, check those out later to see what might work best for you based on your personality.

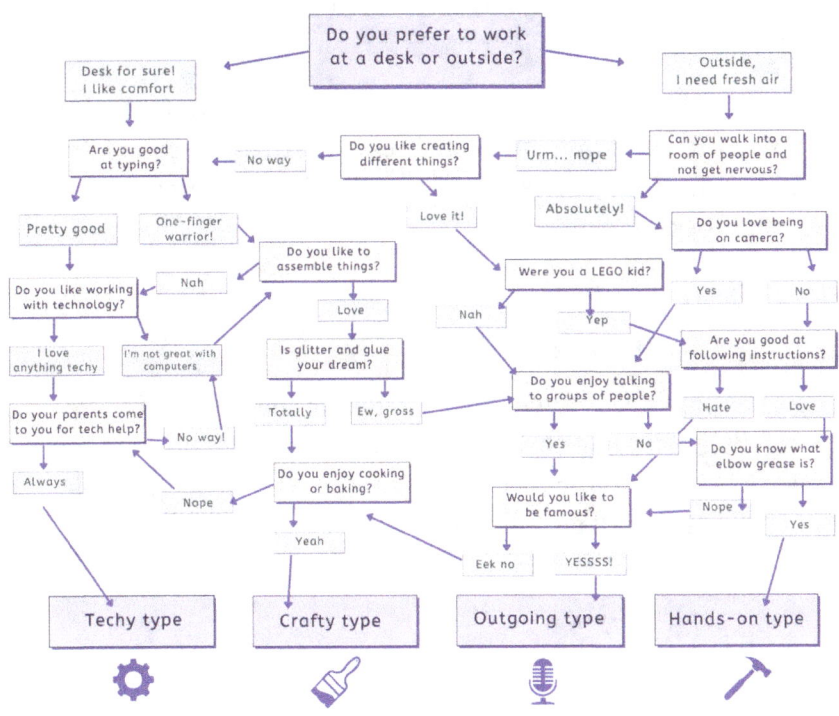

Step one – Discover your big idea

Brainstorming ideas

Now that you've identified your passions, it's time to write down some business ideas. It can be pretty difficult to choose an idea when you've listed loads of things you love, so it's useful to write them down and pick the best one. And don't worry if you have a few different ideas for each passion – that's a good thing!

Check off these three As to confirm you have a great business idea:

> **A**wesome – Is your idea unique enough to stand out in a crowded marketplace? It doesn't have to be a brand-new invention. However, it does have to be different enough to attract interest, and make people want to buy.
>
> **A**ppealing – Does your business appeal to enough people to make it successful? It needs to appeal to the people in *your niche*.
>
> **A**chievable – Can you actually make this business? There's no point in dreaming up a business idea that you can't afford or that needs products that are impossible to source (like moon rocks or tropical fish).

UNLEASH YOUR NICHE

Niche (pronounced 'neesh' – or 'nitch', for our American friends): When you choose a specific group of people who you want to sell your product or service to, it's called finding your niche. It's a small part of a larger target market (group).

Examples:

My passions	Biz idea	Who would buy it?	Is it awesome?	Is it appealing?	Is it achievable?
Dogs	Dog walking	Dog owners	It's OK, but there are a few similar businesses around	Yes, there are lots of dog owners in my town, so it would appeal to many	Yes, I could set this up easily around my neighbourhood
Dogs	Customised rainbow dog collars	Dog owners	Yes, the designs are unique	Yes, people seem to love these, and I can post them anywhere	Yes, I have made these before and can buy the products easily for little upfront cash
Sustainability	'Green' home consultant	People interested in sustainable living	It's a good idea for people who are interested in saving the planet	People might prefer to get this info online	Not really, as I couldn't do this alone for safety; I'd need Mum's help
Sustainability	Upcycling furniture	People who like unique furniture	Each piece is totally unique, so it is awesome as it's one of a kind	Yes, to people who like this style	Not really, I could get free furniture from the council to clean up or from marketplace, but Mum would have to help me talk to people online and pick stuff up

Have a go at writing your own list to see what business ideas you can come up with. It's sometimes easier to bounce ideas off someone else for this, so if you're stuck, have a chat with your friends or family to get their input.

Once you've made your list, you'll see some ideas have more pros and cons than others. Choosing what idea you think will work best doesn't have to be overly complicated. If you love it, take a chance and give it a go!

Local vs global

Something to bear in mind when weighing up the pros and cons is that an online business is immediately more easily scalable than something that only works in your suburb. So, if you're selling something locally, it's good to look at how to expand later. Could you post your product nationwide? Could you run online classes? Could customers download their product?

Making millions!

Another thing to note in entrepreneurship is that any business can be scaled up as big as you like. To make your business blow up (a million-dollar business and beyond), you can't keep trading your time for money. If you're dog walking, you can only walk so many pups in a day! Scaling up your business means you stop trading *your* time for money and, instead, you start managing the process and hiring other people to trade *their* time for money. So, instead of being the dog walker, you manage a dog-walking team. Then you can have a dog-walking team in each suburb, then in each state and beyond. But we're getting a little ahead of ourselves here. Let's get your biz up and running before you take over the world!

Pick your business idea and let's get to the next step...

Quick chapter recap

1. Your business must be in **something you are passionate about.**

2. Your business should **solve a problem** for someone.

3. You must know what your **business niche** is.

4. Your business must be **awesome, appealing and achievable.**

5. **Any business can grow** and expand. There are lots of ways to do this.

CHAPTER 4

Step two – Research and test

You've picked your business idea and made sure it's awesome, appealing and achievable. Pat on the back! Now, before you go full steam ahead and build your biz, there are a few more steps to follow. One of the most important parts is *research*. It might sound boring, but trust me, research is the *secret weapon* for successful entrepreneurs.

A huge mistake many people make when starting a business is not doing any quality research in the beginning – and this can be an absolute killer.

The thing is, just because YOU think you have a great idea, doesn't necessarily mean other people will think the same. I mean, my kid loves to eat ice cream on hot chips, but I don't see many ice cream sauce options at the chip shops, do you?

It might sound obvious, but a business *must* make, or do, something that people actually *want*. Otherwise, your biz will last about as long as that ice cream on the hot chips!

Finding out what people want

How do I find out if people actually want what I'm selling? Great question; there are a few ways, but the most obvious is to ask them.

Chatting to people is the easiest way to find out what they want and a great way to build your communication skills. You can start by asking your own friends and family, and then once you get more confident, ask your neighbours, teachers, community and other people outside of your friendship groups.

PEOPLE TO ASK

Don't forget to ask people you don't know. This is an important step as your friends and family will often tell you what you want to hear to encourage you, but you need to hear the truth. Think of it like trying out a new hairstyle. Your best friend might tell you that you look amazing, but that might be because they don't want to hurt your feelings. However, a stranger on the street would let you know it doesn't suit you, and that's the kind of honest feedback you're after.

By asking enough people questions (aim for at least 10-20 people) about your business idea, you will get a pretty good idea of what they want and don't want. So, what do you actually ask them? Well, it depends on your business, but your aim is to discover if your product, or service, solves the problem they have.

Solve it!

You don't have to overthink this. An umbrella solves the problem of getting wet outside and a band aid solves the problem of getting dirt in a wound. Cordless headphones solve the problem of tangled wires and a restaurant solves the problem of having to cook at home... You get it? You just need to know what the customer's problem is, then you can solve it for them. Easy!

Perfect problem solvers

There are so many great examples of businesses that have identified a problem, successfully solved it and created an unstoppable business venture. Check out these for true inspiration:

- **Netflix.** Netflix solved so many problems for people, it's no wonder it became a success. Using that awesome remote meant no more costly rental services, no more late-night trips to the DVD store, no more organising your life around when you could rent a particular video. Not to mention no more late fees. It's hardly a surprise that everyone developed such a Netflixation.

- **Rent the Runway.** Traditional shopping meant that so many people couldn't afford new designer clothes, but Jenn Hyman and Jenny Fleiss changed all of that when they founded Rent the Runway (RTR). It meant no more spending a fortune on an outfit for an event, no more worrying about trends, no more endless trawling the shops. Simply rent your clothes online for a budget-friendly price!

- **Airbnb.** Airbnb spotted a problem with the cost of travel and accommodations, so it came up with a solution – affordable and unique places to stay all over the world. Like having a home away from home! This type of business model or 'sharing economy' is now very popular worldwide.

Now, have a go at identifying how your biz would be solving a problem for your customers.

RECAP – HOW TO MAKE AN AWESOME BUSINESS

- Identify a problem
- Solve that problem
- Successfully communicate to the customer how your product or service solves the problem better than anyone else. BOOM! You got yourself a rad biz!

Survey day

OK, back to finding out what people want. Asking them is great, but it's easy to forget the key questions when you are chatting with them. A survey or form is a great way to keep on track. Here is an example:

Name _____

Address _____

How often does your lawn need mowing?
_____

Do you mow your own lawn?
_____

If not, what company do you use?
_____

How much would you pay for your lawn to be mowed?
_____

Do you have any special lawn needs?
_____

Can I send you some information when I start my own business?
_____

What is your email address?
_____

Thanks!

More research

There are more ways to have a look at what people want:

#1 Check popular keywords or phrases on search engines

Did you know you can check the most popular questions asked globally about any given topic on search engines like Google or Bing? A popular website for this is *answerthepublic.com*.

It's simple to use – type in a word, and it will provide you with the most common searches related to that word. For example, if I wanted to design and sell yoga shorts, I would type in 'yoga shorts', and it would show me the top questions people are asking in searches, such as 'yoga shorts with pockets' or 'waterproof yoga shorts'.

This gives you fantastic insight into what people are looking for and the problems they want to solve. Using this data, you would make sure your yoga shorts have pockets and are made from waterproof material, having learnt that's what people are looking for.

#2 Forums

Another way to research what people want is looking at online forums and chat threads. These platforms provide valuable real-time research and can offer a wealth of information. Just remember to use these sites with an adult to monitor content and ensure you stay safe online.

Taking advice with a grain of salt

Asking people what they want is fab and really helps you get a feel for what they like. However, remember that you don't have to do everything they say. When it comes down to it, all ideas are subjective.

The key is to get enough info to give you an idea, but that's as far as you need to go.

There's a famous quote from Henry Ford (the guy who developed the Ford Model T automobile): "If I had asked people what they wanted, they would have said faster horses." The moral of the story is that the customer sometimes doesn't have a clue about what they want until they see it, and once they've seen it, they want it! I mean, think about it. Did anyone really think they needed a phone that could also take videos, play music, store photos, give them directions and search the World Wide Web? Nope! But once the smartphone came out, suddenly everyone couldn't live without it.

Know your enemy!

Next, you need to research your enemy, and when I say enemy, what I mean is *competition*.

Your competition is the other businesses that work in your space. Using the survey example, it would be the other lawn-mowing businesses in your area. There's always going to be someone else in your space, and it's not about taking them down, it's about knowing what they're doing, and how you can do it better. It's about being the best *you* can be.

Research your rivals

You may have gathered a few competitor business names when doing your surveys or googling what's out there. This is a great place to start researching your competition. Have a look online and check out what they are doing. Take a peek at what they offer – do they have any special services? Is there anything they are not doing? Is there something you could do differently to stand out? Have a look at their pricing to see what they are charging. This will give you an idea of what people expect and give you a starting point.

Checking out your competitor's social media pages to see what they are posting is also useful for checking out their branding, business name and logo. You want to ensure you don't come up with the same name by mistake. Don't get swamped in competitor research, though – you want to know what's happening, but ensure you spend most of your energy on your own business.

Testing your product or service

Now is a great time to test your product or service. You already know that it's something you like doing, but you want to test if it's any good before you build a whole business around it. Testing your product allows you to see if it works the way it's supposed to, and if people actually like it.

Let's say you want to make a cupcake business because you are a brilliant baker. Well, you need to ensure that you test out your recipes first. There's no point in making a whole batch of broccoli cupcakes if no one wants to buy them.

Cupcake flavours would have been part of your survey and earlier research, so you should have something to work on.

A fair test

When asking people to test your product, it's extremely important not to sway or influence their opinion so that the results can be genuine. When handing out the cupcakes, don't say, "This one has the best ingredients" or "My mum says this one is gross" as you'll sway their opinion. Just keep schtum and let the results speak for themselves.

You'll have to spend some money upfront to make your test products. This will be money well spent, believe me. You should also try to think about your products carefully to make them different from your competitors. Can you use local ingredients to support a local farm? Is there an option to only use low-allergy products? Can you make them a unique shape or size?

Stand out!

By making your products unique, you will differentiate yourself from the competition. Knowing what makes your business unique is important. This is called your Unique Selling Point (or USP). It's what makes you stand out from the crowd and is the sweet spot of offering what the customer wants, what you know you do well and what the competition lacks.

Sometimes it's difficult to think of what your USP is, especially if your business is similar to others out there. But it's important to identify your USP as it will help you sell your product better later on.

Brands and their USPs

Starbucks

In a sea of coffee shops, how do you stand out? While every coffee shop says it sells great coffee, Starbucks has made itself unique by selling a 'coffee experience'. It has nailed the endless fancy coffee options, social media photo opportunities and connecting to its customers by writing names on coffee orders.

Apple

Apple stands out with its sleek design and user-friendly technology. People say they love Apple products because they're easy to use and look great, which makes everyone want a piece of the (apple) pie. (See what I did there?)

Burger King

Differentiating itself from other fast-food places, Burger King focuses on fast tasty food, but with a strong emphasis on good ingredients and 'having it your way', in your own style.

> Did you know that Burger King is called Hungry Jacks in Australia? It's the only place in the world it has a different name. The name Burger King was already trademarked when it entered Australia, so it chose a different name instead.

Quick chapter recap

1. Your business **must** make, or do, something people want.

2. You can **find out what people want** by asking them and doing research.

3. Your business must **solve a problem.**

4. You should always **research your competition.**

5. It is essential to **test your product** or service.

6. Identifying **what makes you unique** (USP) helps you stand out.

CHAPTER 5

Step three – Establish a business plan

You've picked your business idea and done your research – carefully sifting through the valuable feedback and brushing off the other stuff.

You've now reached the next step – shaping your business plan.

There are heaps of things you can add to a business plan, but for now, I'm going to get you to focus on four things only. This four-point business plan is so you can get a crystal-clear idea in your head. For your business, you need to be able to describe the following points:

1. **What** are you selling? (What's your product or service?)
2. **Where** are you selling it? (Location, location, location.)
3. **Who** are you selling to and how are you telling them? (This is called advertising, and there's a whole chapter on this, so we'll get stuck in soon.)
4. **How** will you make money from it? (Monetising.)

By focusing on these simple four key points and understanding them completely, you'll be better prepared for what lies ahead.

Albert Einstein said, "If you can't explain it to a six-year-old, then you don't understand it yourself." So, if you can't summarise your business in these four points easily, then you can't expect anyone else to understand it either. It's vital you nail this part!

Create your own business plan so you have everything covered. Here are some examples so you can see how this works...

WHAT are you selling? (Product/service)	**WHERE** are you selling it? (Location)	**WHO** are you selling to and how will you tell them? (Advertising)	**HOW** will you make money from it? (Monetising)
Bead necklaces for teething babies	On a market stall at my local Saturday farmers' market	Parents with babies and adults buying gifts for parents; I will promote through the farmers' market Facebook page	I will collect cash and card payments on the stall
Clay stud earrings	Etsy website	Selling to anyone with pierced ears and people buying gifts; I will advertise on my own socials, local flyers and use Etsy ads	Payments will be processed through the Etsy website
Monthly crafting kits for kids	Through my website	The kits are for 5- to 10-year-olds, so I will be selling to their parents; I will advertise online and through my school newsletter	Through a subscription service – people pay a monthly fee and are sent a different box each month

Next, you'll take your simple four-point business plan and break it down into sections to extend the set-up:

1. WHAT are you selling? *(What's your product or service?)*

Breaking this part down is pretty simple. You already know what you are selling, *and* you've identified the problem you're solving. That's A+ work right there!

Features and benefits

I'm going to get you to take this a step further and work out the *features* and *benefits* of your product or service. This will make it a hundred times easier for you to sell your product.

It's easy to get mixed up between features and benefits, so here's an easy way to remember: Features TELL, Benefits SELL.

What is she on about? I hear you ask. Well, before you write this off as gobbledegook, let me explain a bit more clearly:

- Features describe what a product or service does or has.
- Benefits highlight a reason the customer would buy it.

Why does it matter?

Knowing what your features and benefits are is crucial. This information enables you to communicate how your product or service helps to meet a customer's needs and solves their problems. And this is key to getting them to buy what you're selling.

Let me give you an example from when the first iPod was sold. This was a product I can remember as one of the most influential pieces of technology to be released at the time (and I couldn't wait to get my hands on one!). This little device changed the path of the music industry and technology as we know it today.

The *features* of the iPod were that it had a 5GB hard drive, rotating scroll wheel and a syncing port. *What does all of that even mean?*

The *benefit*, on the other hand, was that you could store every song you could ever wish to on that one little device. In fact, when he first showed it to audiences, Steve Jobs famously said, "1,000 songs in your pocket". SOLD! Take my money, Apple!

You get it? Features *tell*, benefits *sell*.

It's all about a good night's sleep!

There's a famous saying in sales: 'Sell the good night's sleep and not the mattress'. It means that people buy the outcome they desire (the *benefit*) over the features. In this case, what they desire is a good night's sleep. Customers don't care about *features* (like how many coils the mattress has). But they DO care about getting a good night's sleep. That's the whole reason they are buying it. Communicating the *benefit* is a skill you shouldn't snooze at!

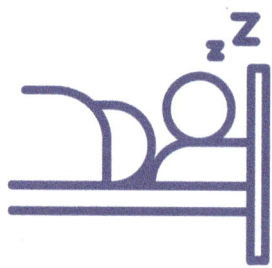

Check out these examples so you get an idea of features and benefits. Then have a go at writing down your own for your product or service...

FEATURES	BENEFITS
Backpack *(product)*	
1. Made from sturdy material 2. Adjustable straps 3. Has six different sections	1. Built to withstand wear and tear so it lasts for a long time 2. Making it easier and more comfortable to carry 3. Easy organisation
Garden care *(service)*	
1. Only uses eco-friendly/green products 2. Open seven days 3. Services can be booked online	1. Better for the customers' health and the environment 2. Can fit in easily with customers' schedules 3. Customers can easily book any time from their phone or computer

Knowing what you are selling is about knowing more than simply what the physical product is. It's about knowing what problem you are solving and what benefits the customer will gain by buying it.

Step three – Establish a business plan

2. WHERE are you selling it? *(Location)*

There are quite a few places you can sell your product or service, and you can likely expand into more than one of these categories. I've mentioned before about scaling your business up to offer online or global options, but there's also nothing wrong with sticking to a local market. Let's take a look at the options…

Market stalls

Setting up a market stall is one of the easiest ways to kick off your business and it's great fun chatting to customers face-to-face. You can often do this outside your own house without any permits. It's the way most young entrepreneurs start, with a simple lemonade stand or garage sale.

You can expand on this to farmers' markets and school or craft fairs. You'll need a table or somewhere to display your wares and a waterproof cover. You may need to rent the space, apply for a permit and have insurance when attending markets in your area. And make sure you have multiple ways for people to pay, if possible, as not everyone carries cash and you won't want to miss out on those sales!

Door to door

This means going directly to people's homes and knocking on the door to sell your product. People are generally quite welcoming, especially when they see a kid trying their best to start a business venture. You just want to make sure you do this with an adult and in an area you both feel comfortable.

Local stores

Approaching local stores around your neighbourhood is a great way to display and sell your products. Just remember that they will want to sell your products to their customers for the same rate you do. That means you'll have to sell your product to the store at a cheaper rate. This is 'wholesale' pricing and we'll delve into this further in this chapter.

Online

There are heaps of existing online platforms you can use to sell your own products. These platforms offer you the chance to showcase your products in a space where customers are already looking to buy. The beauty of using an online platform is that it's already set up, meaning you don't have to create a website or shopping cart from scratch. Some online platforms to sell your items include Etsy, eBay, Amazon, Facebook Marketplace or Gumtree for local sales.

Website

Another way to utilise the online world is to create your own website. This will take a little longer to set up in the beginning, and you'll want to ensure it looks professional by using high-quality graphics, photos and designs. It's well worth the effort in the long run. A professional website works wonders for your sales and is available for your customers to view at any time of day. Most platforms require users to be over 18, so your biz partner can do this.

Social media

Social media platforms are a popular way to promote most products. You can also use the platforms to sell your products. You can link your socials pages to your shop or website, and you can also sell in your community on a localised marketplace. Remember your safety here!

3. WHO are you selling to and how are you telling them? *(Advertising)*

The group of people who will most likely buy your product or service is called a 'target market'. It's important you have an idea of who you are going to sell to. Knowing your target market is extremely important.

Imagine you're selling dog collars. You don't want to be wasting all your time, money and energy at the fish market or outside baby stores trying to sell dog collars. It wouldn't be a good business move. You need to know your target market to know where to find them. Pawfect!

Target market = The group of people who will most likely buy what you're selling.

Niche = A smaller section of your target market that has more specific needs.

Examples:

The target market could be pet owners, but your niche could be dog owners. OR

The target market could be gamers, but your niche could be Nintendo gamers.

Target customer

When identifying your target customer, you need to know everything about them: their likes, dislikes, where they hang out; and find their information: where they live plus anything else you can think of.

To do this, it's a great idea to create your own customer avatar. A customer avatar is like creating a special character that represents your ideal customer. It's a way to understand the type of person who would be interested in your product or service. Once you get a clear idea of your customer, it will help you work out how you are going to tell them about your business. This means you can create better advertising materials, targeted to them. You can name your avatar to keep them in mind whenever you think about what you are selling and where to advertise.

I've created an example below of a customer avatar you might create for a local pet photography business.

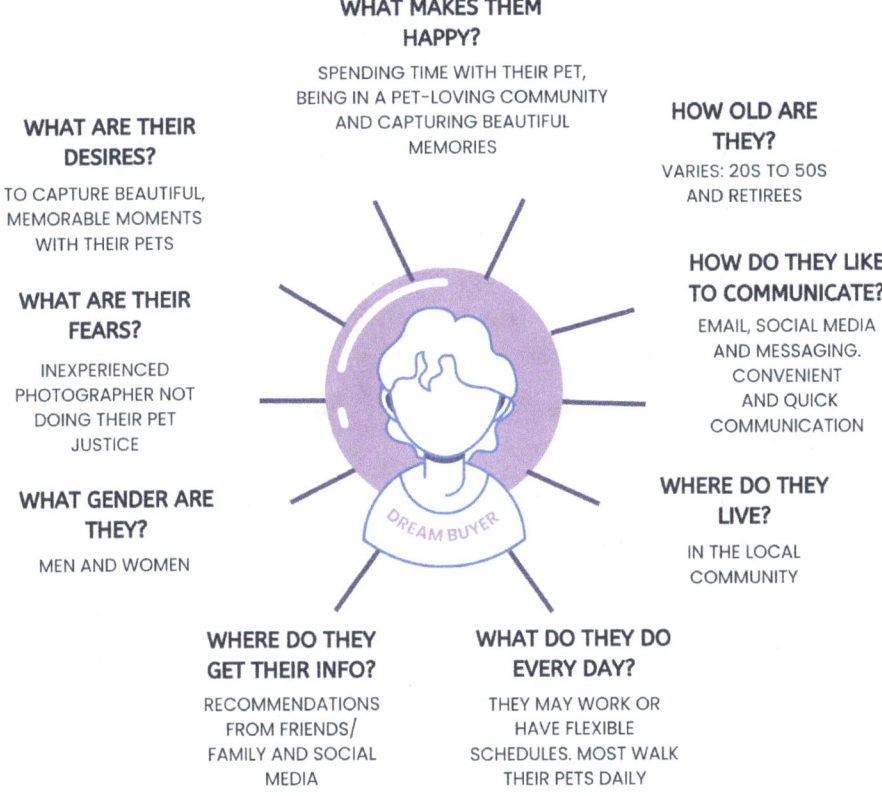

Have a go at creating your own customer avatar for your business.

Step three - Establish a business plan   **45**

Let's recap, so this bit is crystal clear...

You need to know your target market, so you know who to try to sell to. A couple of examples of this would be:

- If you sell sports sneakers for adults, you aren't going to try to sell them to kids. Your target market would be adults interested in fitness.
- If you sell lemonade outside your house, then you aren't going to advertise it in another town. Your target market would be people in your neighbourhood who might like a drink.

Zooming in on your niche

Now here is some uber-cool next-level business learning. When you get going with your business, you can level up by zooming in on a certain section of people within your target market. This is your niche. This doesn't need to happen at the beginning; you can get a clearer idea of this as you progress and narrow it down as you get more familiar with your biz.

Using the same examples we used for our target market, we can zoom in to discover a niche:

- For the sports sneaker business, your niche could be more eco-conscious customers with a product line made entirely of recycled material.
- With the lemonade stand, your niche could be offering sugar-free lemonade or fruit-infused juice to cater to health-conscious people, making you stand out from regular lemonade stands.

4. HOW will you make money from it?
(Monetising)

A successful business will make a profit. That's the whole point! So, it's crucial you will be able to work out how you are going to make money, and what to do with the money. This bit comes later.

First, you need to be sure you understand how to make a profit. Let's start from the top – what exactly is a profit?

Making a profit

Your PROFIT is what's left over after all your bills have been paid.

The money coming IN to your business must be more than the money going OUT. You might think this is the most obvious thing in the world, but honestly, I've met grown adults working in sales who still don't truly grasp this. It makes me wonder how they got that far, I tell you!

To work out your profit, you make a budget that captures all your income and expenses.

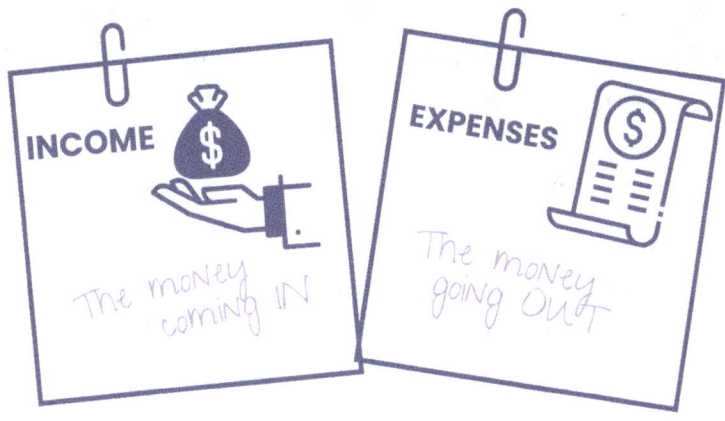

Income vs expenses

Let's take a look at what your income and expenses are.

Income is the money coming IN.

> If you're selling a **product**, like doughnuts, your income is how many items you sell, multiplied by the price.

You would work out your expected income on a doughnut stall as this:

- You expect to sell 60 doughnuts a day.
- Your doughnuts cost $4 each.

60 x $4 = **$240 a day.** Not bad!

If you ran your doughnut stall every single Saturday in a month (assuming there are four Saturdays in that month), then you could expect to get **$960 income per month** ($240 a day multiplied by 4).

> If you're selling a **service**, like babysitting, your income is what you would charge per hour, multiplied by the number of hours you would expect to work.

You would work this out like so:

- You charge $20 an hour
- You babysit every Friday and Saturday night each month

Your shifts run for three hours each time. Assuming there were four weekends that month, you would make $480 per month.

$20 per hour x 3 = $60 per shift.
Multiplied by eight shifts = **$480 a month.**

Expenses are the money going OUT.

These are the actual *costs* of running your business. These costs can really mount up, so don't forget to make a list of them as you go. Weekly supplies are front of mind, but it's easy to forget things like website hosting fees or the amount you spent on printing flyers or posters.

Tip: when it comes to big-ticket items, like a doughnut machine to make those mouth-watering doughnuts, make sure you spread the cost out over a longer period. You would only need to buy one machine upfront, so you could spread the cost over the *hole* first year (see what I did there?). If your machine costs $420, you could borrow the *dough* from your awesome grandma to pay for it, then you would divide that by 12 months and pay her back $35 a month. Easy-peasy!

Now, the moment of truth! When you subtract all those expenses from your total income figure, you'll reveal the real deal. Are you making a profit or ending up in the negative?

Let's look at the examples I've just given in this budget template:

Doughnut stall (product-based business)

Monthly expenses	
Doughnut machine (repay Gran)	$35
Ingredients	$280
Cutters	$20
Towels and cleaning supplies	$30
Total	**$365**

Monthly income			
Product sold	Price per unit	Amount sold per month	Total income
Pink-glazed doughnuts	$4	104	$416
White-glazed doughnuts	$4	136	$544
Total income			**$960**
Minus total expenses			-$365
Total monthly profit			**$595**

Babysitting business (service-based business)

Monthly expenses	
Walking to each house	$0
Total	**$0**

Monthly income					
Service/ bookings	Booking per week	Hours	Cost per hour	$ per week	$ per month
Number 7 Smith Street	1 (every Friday night)	3	$20	$60	$240
Number 4 Wallace Street	1 (every Saturday night)	3	$20	$60	$240
Total income					**$480**
Minus total expenses					-$0
Total monthly profit					**$480**

With these examples, you can see that you make more money per month with the doughnut business. The doughnut business might give you more profit, but the time invested is greater. AND you haven't factored in your time – everyone forgets this part!

If you spent eight hours a day working on your doughnut stall each week, that would mean you would be spending 32 hours working in your doughnut stall each month (8 hours x 4 Saturdays).

With your $595 profit, if you divide that by the hours worked (595 / 32), we can see you actually made $18.59 per hour.

Based on our hourly fee, it would seem the babysitting job is the more profitable option.

One side of the coin

Trading your time for money is only one side of the coin, though. If your passion is doughnuts, don't give up yet! Remember, it's vital you work in what you are passionate about and there are plenty of ways to grow that biz. You could use your knowledge in other ways to grow your income such as creating an eBook of doughnut recipes. Or you could work on a way of reducing expenses, so your profit is increased. Just ensure you don't sacrifice your product quality to make a profit.

Cash or card

When you know your business idea has profit potential, you'll need to set up a clear way of accepting payments. If you're cash only, that's OK, but you might miss out on sales. By setting up a way for people to pay using their bank card, it will make the process easy for the customer. Believe me, it HAS to be easy!

Have a go at creating your own budget to ensure you can make a decent profit once you get going.

Pricing your product

You've worked out your budget and estimated profit per month. Well done – that part required a bit of concentration! But how do you know you are charging the correct amount for your product?

If you're not making a profit, then perhaps your 'sell' price is not high enough. Pricing your product or service is a crucial part of your business plan. Here are a few ways you can check you have the right pricing:

1. Calculate your costs

By working out all the costs involved in producing your product (your expenses), you can easily ensure you're earning a profit. You want to make sure you have a good profit margin on top of the total cost. For example, if it cost you $5 to make a keyring and you sell it for $10, your profit is $5. Don't forget to factor in your time, though!

2. Research your competitors

By having a look at similar products and businesses in your area, you will get a good idea of the going rate. This will help you price your products competitively.

3. Supply and demand

If there is a high demand for your product (meaning loads of people want it), and you only have a few items to sell (such as one-off artwork), then you can set your pricing higher.

Also, look at what value you bring – if your product or service solves a significant problem, then customers may be willing to pay more for it. If you are the only lemonade stand on a scorching day at a festival, then people will likely pay more for your product. You don't want to rip people off, though (this is called 'price gouging'). However, it's important to recognise the value you bring.

The opposite happens when there is an oversupply (too many lemonade stands) and not enough people wanting to buy lemonade (low demand). Then you'll find it hard to sell anything.

4. Know who you're selling to

This is vital to work out pricing – especially knowing the difference between selling to the end customer or selling to a shop. Let me break it down...

Imagine you have a cool jewellery biz. You might sell directly to customers or to shops. When you sell to a shop, it's called 'wholesale'. This bit is important to remember: the shop will buy your products for a price cheaper than what they plan to sell them for. The price they will sell it for is known as the 'recommended retail price' (RRP).

Let's take the keychain example:

It costs you $5 to make each keychain, factoring in your time and materials. You've been selling them to friends and family for $10, which is great!

Then a local shop contacts you. It wants to stock your fantastic keychains – how awesome is that? But here's the catch: the shop wants to sell them for the same price you've been selling them for, which is $10. They'll ask to buy the keychains from you for less than $10. Usually (not always, but often), shops expect the wholesale price to be half of what the selling price is. So, they'll want to buy your keychains for $5.

You realise that if you sell to the shop at that price, you won't make any profit at all. But don't worry, there's a solution! You can set your RRP higher, at $20. That way, you can still sell them wholesale to the shop for $10 and make a sweet $5 profit! You must get this pricing strategy right from the beginning. People won't want the RRP to suddenly increase for no reason.

Understanding your target market and pricing strategy can make a huge difference in your success as a young entrepreneur.

5. Niche pricing

We've already explored your target market – the group of people you want to reach; and niche – the small, unique segment within your target market. Now I'm going to delve into why understanding your niche can have an impact on your pricing.

Knowing your niche is essential for pricing your products or services. Let me explain. Imagine you offer a dog-grooming service. Your target market is made up of dog owners, and you've set your grooming costs at $80 for a small dog and $100 for a large dog.

But hold up, let's introduce the niche! Suppose you decide to focus on offering high-end, premium dog-grooming services. In this case, your niche becomes 'premium dog grooming'. As a result, your pricing must reflect this exclusive experience you offer (hint – your pricing must increase!).

Now, a small dog-grooming session wouldn't be just $80 anymore. Instead, it would be a luxury experience, complete with upscale grooming in a spa-like setting. Your customers would gladly pay more for this lavish service for their furry friends. As you can see, identifying your niche means you can tailor your offerings to a specific group of customers who value the unique experiences you provide. So, when you're clear about your niche, you can adjust your pricing to match (often making them quite a lot higher!).

Quick chapter recap

1. You should have a **clear business plan**.

2. You need to understand the **features and benefits** for the customer of what you're selling.

3. You should have a clear idea of who your **target market** is and understand your **niche**.

4. It is important you have **your pricing worked out**.

5. You should know if you are going to **make a profit**.

CHAPTER 6

Step four – Advertise your business

You've picked your biz idea, done your research, established a business plan AND worked out that you can make money. I'm sure you're totally revved up to get this going now, so let's get moving!

Next, we need to look at advertising. And to advertise your biz, you need to nail your branding.

Advertising and branding

What is advertising and branding? Advertising is simply getting people interested in what you are selling. It's about getting the word out there and telling people about your product or service. Branding is about creating a look, or an identity, for your business. One that makes you stand out from the crowd. So, the first thing you need to do is create your unique brand identity.

Business name

First things first, you need a business name – I know you've been thinking about this! There are lots of things to consider when it comes to thinking of your business name:

1. **It should give people a hint about what your business is about.** If you have a local cleaning service, don't call it 'Purple Lollies' as people need an idea of what you do. You could call it 'Shiny Spaces House Cleaning', then people are more likely to find it when searching it online. (This is called Search Engine Optimisation (SEO) and it is important to consider when thinking up a name.)

2. **It should be easy to remember.** Making your name catchy and easy to pronounce is important. Simple is key.

3. **Is it unique?** You don't want your biz name to be too similar to other businesses out there. Make it as special as you are.

4. **Ensure there are no legal or trademark issues** and remember to check your domain is available for your website and socials handles.

Business name ideas

Your biz name could be your real name, a compound (two words put together), an acronym, an abbreviation or even a made-up word!

Here are some examples:

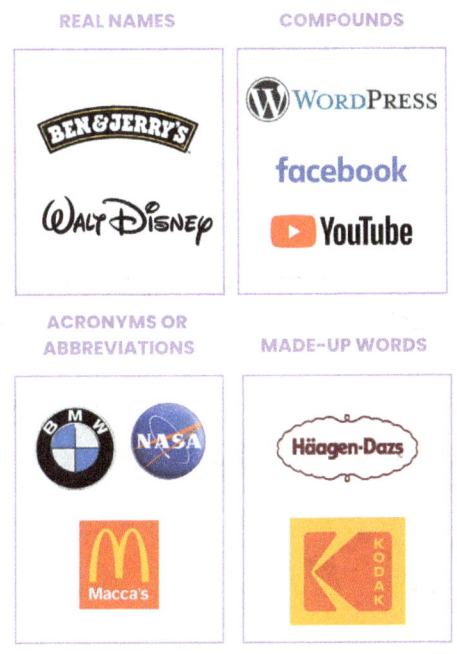

Consider your company values, your favourite things, nicknames, your inspirations or even puns! A pun is a joke that makes a play on words. You will have seen loads of business names that use puns. Hairdressers, barber shops and fish and chip shops often use them.

Some punny examples:

 Cake My Day (cake shop)

 The Codfather (fish and chip shop)

 Jabba the Cut (hairdresser)

 Knead it! (bakery)

Business logo and branding

Once you have your biz name, you can get totally creative designing your business logo. A great logo helps people recognise – and remember – your brand.

Your logo should be:

- Simple
- Memorable
- Versatile
- Relevant

I bet you recognise every single one of these famous logos, from the swoosh of the Nike tick to the golden arches of the Macca's logo:

Before you jump straight in with your logo design, let's chat about logo colours. Believe it or not, there's a whole psychology behind choosing a colour for your logo. It might sound strange, but colours stimulate different emotions, catch your eye and even influence your behaviour!

Some colour options are easy to consider. For instance, if your product is an all-natural eco product, you might consider a green logo to represent nature. Or if your product is youthful and fun, you might choose a bright, bold colour.

Take a look at the chart below to check out what each colour represents and consider this when creating your own branding:

Step four – Advertise your business

Remember to use your business name and logo to give people an idea of what you are selling, and add some personality, too. I've brainstormed a few biz names below to get your creative juices flowing. Take a look at these and then design your own...

- Instead of *Alex and Rowan's lemonade stand,* aim for a more unique twist like *The Lil' Lemonade Crew.*
- Instead of *Oscar's Face-painting Service,* aim for a creative name like *Face Paint Fever!*
- Instead of *Dog Grooming by Phoebe,* you could have *The Bark Boutique.*

Remember that you will adapt your branding for all other aspects of your packaging and advertising material, so it is a good idea to make the final design on your computer if you can, so you have it as a digital file. Photoshop, Canva and other design platforms are great for this.

Advertising your biz

Now we are going to look at advertising. Getting the word out there can be done in many ways. From online ads, posters, school newsletters, telling people in person or even carrier pigeon – there are many ways to reach people (OK, that last one isn't such a great idea, but these ones opposite are!).

Marketing your biz

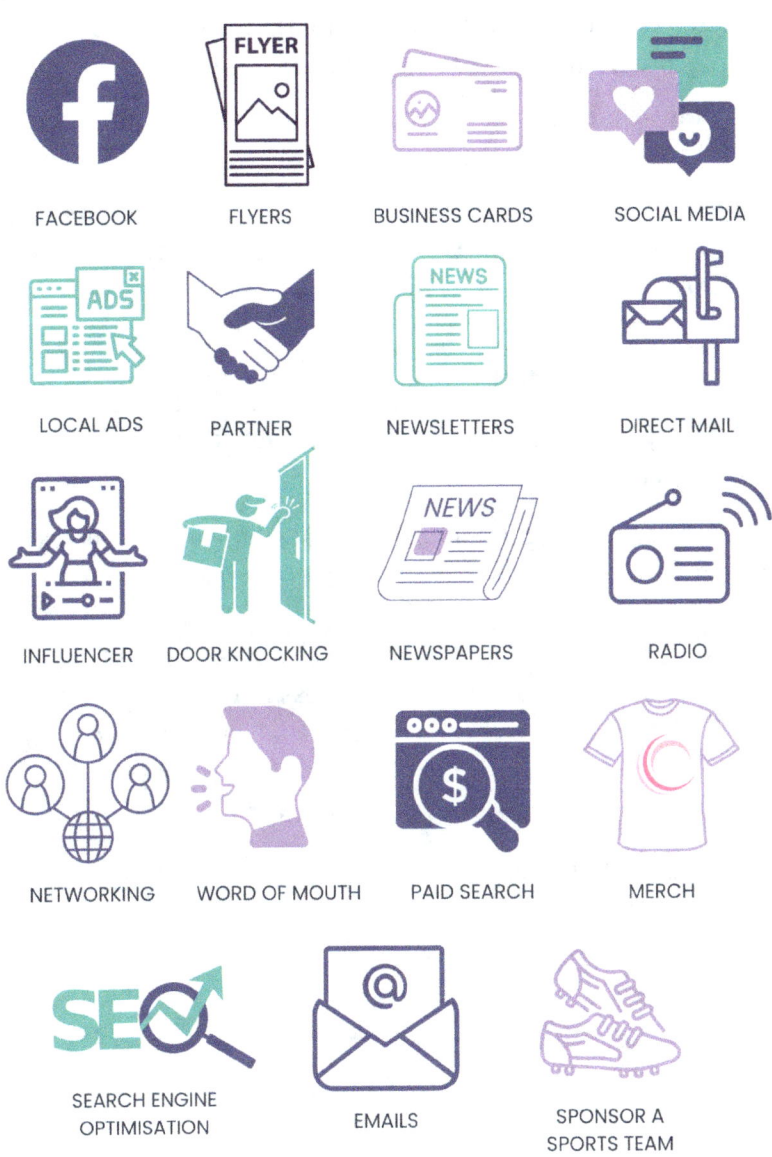

It's all about finding the right way to connect with YOUR target market. You wouldn't advertise your baby food business outside the pet shop, or your walking aids to the local basketball team. That's not where your target market hangs out. It's important to always use your time and money wisely when marketing your biz.

You already worked out where your target market gets its information, so start there, and spread the word.

It's important to understand that different types of advertising suits different types of businesses. Check out these businesses and how they are promoting what they do:

Business/product	Advertising
Local bakery selling freshly baked goods	Local flyers and posters
Trendy online clothing brand aimed at teens	Social media ads on TikTok and Instagram
School fundraising cake stand	School newsletter
Fitness products sold online	Fitness influencer collaboration on social media and wearing their own logo on their merchandise
Local restaurant offering takeaway food	Letterbox drop/direct mail

Word of mouth

Once your business gets going, something incredible starts to happen. People start advertising for you by telling their friends and family about your product or service. This is called 'word-of-mouth' advertising and is one of the best forms of advertising you can get. It's free, genuine and ongoing.

Be sure to keep doing a good job to get this as word of mouth spreads faster when a customer is unhappy!

Creating interest

When you are starting out, you may find you have to get creative to reel customers in. After all, they have never heard of your business, so could be reluctant to try at first. This is where you might need to get inventive by implementing a few strategies to hook them in!

Here are a few ideas you can try to create more interest (but don't try them all at once):

1. Offer a free sample or a special discount or promotion to a new customer.
2. Show you have complete confidence in your product or service by offering a guarantee.
3. Use social media to engage your customer by posting stories or engaging content.
4. Collaborate with someone else to help you reach more customers.
5. Give super awesome customer service so they remember and recommend you.

Designing your own marketing

Have a go at designing your own marketing using this flyer as an example, making sure you include the following:

- Business name and logo
- Clear offering
- Your USP
- A way to reel the customer in or capture their attention
- A clear and simple way to buy your product or service
- Photos if you have them
- Show how you are solving their problem

Talk the talk

To be able to advertise your business, it's important you can talk about it with absolutely anyone. It's essential you understand what your business does and that you can explain it clearly to anyone who asks. Every conversation you have is a possible opportunity. You never know where your next customer might come from.

This brings us to one of my favourite skills of an entrepreneur – mastering your elevator pitch.

Elevator pitch

What exactly is an 'elevator pitch'? In simple terms, it's a brief pitch designed to grab someone's attention and get them excited about your business.

Imagine this: You step into an elevator and in walks Jeff Bezos, the founder of Amazon. You have less than a minute (the time it takes for your elevator to get to the ground floor) to tell this incredibly successful dude about your business. And if you're lucky, he might just take enough of an interest to buy something or even invest!

At that moment, you wouldn't waste time talking about the weather or just shooting the breeze, would you? No! You'd jump straight in there and pitch your biz. Now, while meeting Jeff Bezos might be a dream, an elevator pitch is a real thing. It's a short memorable description of what you do or sell. And nailing this is super important.

You will share your pitch with so many people: investors, customers, teachers, family members and even the media. If you can pitch your business well, the possibilities are endless!

And if you can't explain what your business does, how do you expect anyone else to understand it?

Crafting your elevator pitch is crucial. In that one minute, you should cover these important points:

- What your business is called

- What you offer
- Why it's unique
- How you are different from your competitors
- Benefits for the customer
- Where they can find your product or service

I've given you a template below, so get working on your elevator pitch. Remember, the key is to practise, practise, practise!

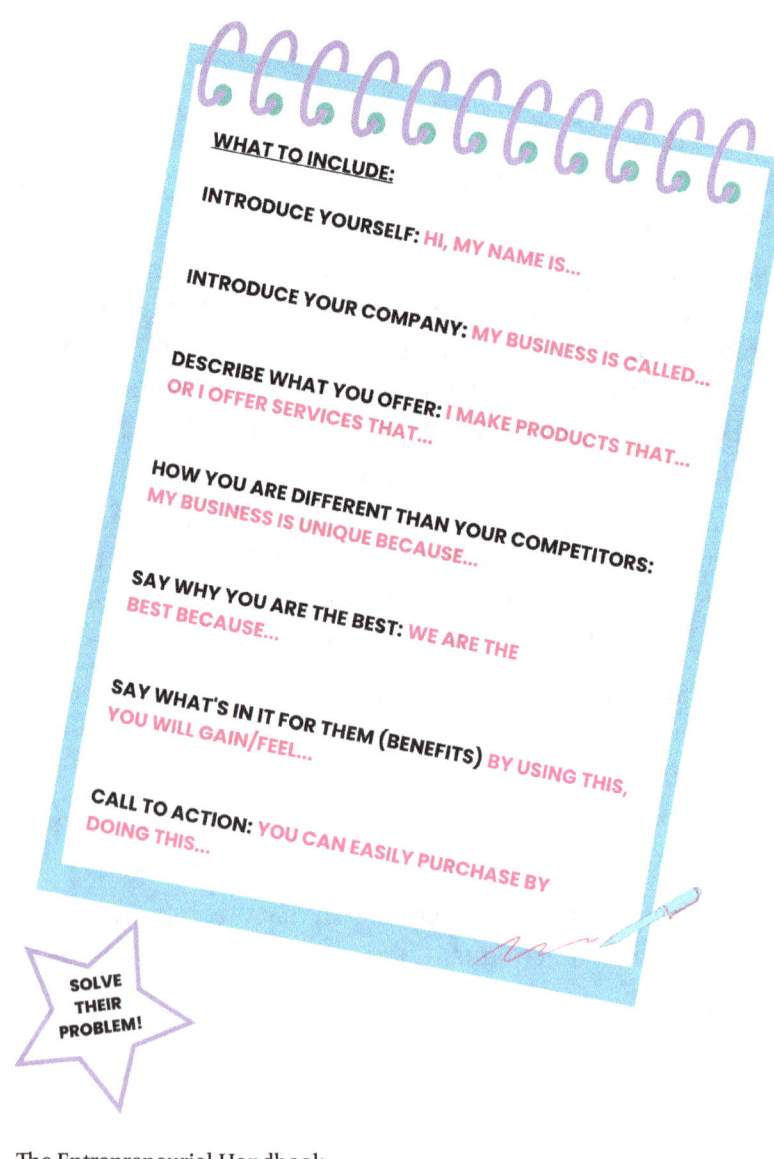

Selling with confidence

One of the most common questions I get asked in my workshops is how to present, and sell, with confidence. If you are going to nail your elevator pitch, then you want to say it with conviction.

Here are some tips to help sell with confidence:

1. **Know your product or service inside and out.** Whether it be all the ingredients, the manufacturing information or what's included in the price – whatever it is, be prepared for any question, so you are confident when talking about it.

2. **Recognise you are helping the customer.** Don't think of it as *selling*, instead, think of it as *helping*.

3. **Speak louder.** When you raise your voice louder when presenting, you sound more confident. Remember to pause, smile and make eye contact. You will look, and sound, like the most confident person in the world – even if you don't feel it. (Just don't start shouting at them!)

4. **Practise, practise, practise.** And practise some more! If you prepare and rehearse as much as possible, you will absolutely win. Put in many hours of practice and you'll totally smash it!

> "Failing to prepare is preparing to fail"
> – Benjamin Franklin

5. **Believe in yourself** – you CAN do this!

Launching

You have planned, researched, tested and developed everything you need to market your business. Now you can either get started softly, building buzz as you go, or you can launch with a bang and have a launch party or event. Launching your business is both exciting and nerve-racking, but you've got this. If you hold a launch party, it is a great way to get some initial sales. Whichever option you choose, the key is to remember to keep momentum long term. Remember, good things take time – building a business takes time – but it's worth it!

Quick chapter recap

1. Your **business name should be clear, easy to remember and catchy.**

2. Your **logo should be strong and simple.**

3. You should **use the correct advertising method** for your potential customers.

4. You can create interest to **reel customers in.**

5. You should **practise your elevator pitch** until you know it off by heart.

6. Once you launch your business, **keep momentum and give it time!**

CHAPTER 7

Step five – Money, money, money!

You've now completed all the steps to get your business up and running and hopefully, you're feeling like the educated entrepreneur you are. You've launched your biz and by this stage, you might be seeing some money coming in. Woohoo! So, what do you do with your money? Hide it under your mattress? Shove it in your moneybox? Bury it in a treasure chest or spend it all on magic beans? I wouldn't recommend the magic beans, that's for sure. Unless your name is Jack...

But I *would* recommend you have a plan.

When I was a young girl, my sweet Nan used to say to me, "Spend half, save half", and I stuck to that rule for many years. I'd have a money pot for spending and a money pot for saving. But growing older, I realised that a couple more pots were needed to make it work.

I now teach the strategy of having four money pots:

- Spend
- Save
- Donate
- Invest

These four money pot ideas are common practice throughout the world; in fact, the idea has been featured in teachings for decades, and there's good reason – it's tried and tested, and it works.

The idea is to allocate a certain percentage to each pot and stick with it. Each time you make a profit, separate your funds into the percentage and add to your pots. (You don't have to actually use 'pots' – you can use jars, boxes, wallets, apps, online platforms or anything else that works for you.)

Let me take you through your pots…

Spend

You work hard on your business and making a profit is a huge deal. Therefore, you deserve to be able to spend some of that hard-earned money! Don't blow it all, though, as that won't help you long term.

Wants vs needs

The trick is to recognise your wants versus your needs.

A *need* is something important that you can't live without, like food, water, clean air or a place to sleep.

A *want* is something you enjoy but can live without, like video games, high-fashion sneakers or a new smartphone.

So, when you're spending that hard-earned cash, consider if you *want* it or *need* it. It's best to make sure you have your needs covered before you think about your wants.

If you need some new clothes, then sure, go buy some (we can't have you walking around naked!). But think smart – you don't need to buy the most expensive items in the shop. If you're hungry and need a snack, then go buy some food. A healthy snack is great, but there's no excuse to buy the whole candy store, even if you want to. Got it?

NECESSARY NEEDS	WISHFUL WANTS
• Shoes	• Designer sneakers
• Books	• New gaming console
• Toothpaste	• Tooth-whitening kits
• Water	• Ultimate milkshake
• Sunshine and fresh air	• Five-star holiday

By thinking smarter, and buying things preowned or more money-smart options, you can get more for your money and stretch that 'spend' pot further.

Save

Saving your money is AWESOME! When you start to see those savings grow, it's a visual representation of how hard you're working. It's a great way to save for a big goal or simply to invest later on. Believe me, it can get quite addictive seeing that little pot get bigger!

Saving is your first step to becoming rich, so keep collecting that moolah!

You can save your cash by stashing it in your moneybox at home or you can use a bank, building society or credit union.

Let me break this down for you:

Banks

A bank is a for-profit place where you can store your cash. They offer different types of services, like savings accounts (where you store your money long term and get interest on your cash), checking accounts (an everyday account for buying lunch or groceries), loans and credit cards. Banks also have shareholders. These are people who own stocks in the banks and benefit from profits made.

Credit unions

A credit union offers similar services to banks, but they are often owned by their members. This means that if you have an account with them, then you own a small part of them. Being smaller, credit unions are often able to give more personal customer service experience and different rates. Credit unions are a not-for-profit financial institution.

Building societies

Building societies are customer-owned institutions, so they are also owned by members. They offer similar services to banks and are often popular for savings and mortgage (home loan) lending.

It's totally up to you which one you join, but it's important to remember that some banks will require a parent or guardian to help you set up your account, and they may have joint ownership. Ages, fees and rates will differ per institution.

The magic of interest

One fab reason to keep your savings in an institution is INTEREST. This is money for nothing.

Whaaaaaaaaaaaaaaaaaaaaaaaat?!

Yup. Money for simply having your money sat in the account. It's only a little amount, but over time it can really make a difference – especially in a savings account where you earn compound interest.

Compound interest

You're in for a treat with this little section of the book. That's because you are going to learn all about the magic of compound interest. Here's the story:

- **Regular interest** is interest based on the amount of money you have in your account (the principal).
- **Compound interest** is the interest you earn on your principal. This is the amount you've put in AND your interest (the amount the bank gives you for putting it into your account). And if you don't think it makes much of a difference, then check this out...

Say you have $1,000 and you put it in the bank, and the (very lovely) bank pays you 10% interest. At the end of the first year, you would have $1,100 in the bank. This is made up of your original $1,000 and $100 extra (10% of 1,000 is 100).

Now, here's where the compound interest magic happens: you make interest on that FULL amount. By the end of the second year, you would have $1,210 (as 10% of 1,100 is 110, so add that to your 1,100 from last year). With each year that goes by, it starts to make a huge difference, as you can see in this table:

Year	Bank balance (at the end of the year)
1	$1,100
2	$1,210
3	$1,331
4	$1,464
5	$1,611
6	$1,772

Starting balance = $1,000

And imagine if you started off with a higher amount. Like $100,000! It would look like this:

Year	Bank balance (at the end of the year)
1	$110,000
2	$121,000
3	$133,100
4	$146,410
5	$161,051
6	$177,156

Starting balance = $100,000

You're making money on your initial principal investment PLUS the interest every year. So, before you go setting up your bank account, ask about compound interest and interest rates. Then make the magic happen!

That should have blown your mind, but there's an extra step that will truly knock your socks off.

In the last examples we saw how much your balance would grow with compound interest based on your initial principal. But what if you added more principal each year? How would this impact your cashola? A ridiculous amount actually!

Check this out:

Year	Your deposit	Bank balance (at the end of the year)
1	$1,000	$1,100
2	$1,000	$2,310
3	$1,000	$3,641
4	$1,000	$5,105
5	$1,000	$6,715
6	$1,000	$8,487

Here you can see you have put $6,000 into your bank account as principal. But with compound interest, you have $8,487 at the end of the sixth year! If you did this for 40 years (investing $1,000 per year), you would have a whopping $242,102!

The bottom line is – open an awesome savings account and keep adding to your savings.

Don't forget to open a separate checking account, too, for spending your money so you can keep these 'money pots' separate.

Examples given utilise a 10% interest rate for ease of teaching purposes; actual interest rates may differ. Please check with your institution prior to setting up an account.

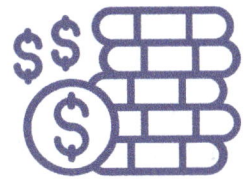

Donate

Did you know that you can have a business reap the rewards and also give some of your money away? Give it AWAY? Yes, you read that correctly.

I know, I know… I've just spent the last six chapters talking about how you must make money and make a profit. And now I'm telling you to… give it away?

Yup.

OK, this section of the book is where we have a heart-to-heart, an honest discussion about the meaning of life. I'm here to tell you that during all my years on Earth, if I've learnt one thing, it is the importance of kindness.

What has this got to do with entrepreneurship, you ask? Well, everything. You see, kindness has a ripple effect. When you make a positive impact on the world and people around you, it spreads beyond what you see. So, you'll understand, when I talk about giving money away, I don't mean all of your money, of course. I mean a percentage that you feel comfortable with donating to a charity or cause to make the world a better place.

If you commit to this regularly, you will see how it not only motivates other people to do the same, but it helps you connect and build relationships within your community. You gain a sense of fulfilment unlike anything else knowing you're genuinely helping someone in need. Kindness is everything.

It's totally up to you where you donate your money and how much you give to your cause. Whether it's 5% or 50%, make sure you allocate this to your *donate* money pot when you work out your profits, and stick to it.

And, of course, if you haven't earned a profit yet, or prefer to give in another way, then you can donate your *time*. By volunteering your time to help your cause, you see all the amazing benefits, and there's no end to what you can do!

CHARITIES OR CAUSES YOU CAN DONATE TO

- Disaster relief
- Animal rescue
- Homelessness
- Children's welfare
- Cancer research
- Environmental conservation
- Literacy programs
- Clean water projects
- Elderly care
- Arts and cultural projects

There are so many more, just find what matters to you!

Invest

Investing is your ultimate superpower when it comes to levelling up. And here's the thing… there is more than one way to invest. I'm going to break this down into three parts for you:

1. **Investing in YOU.**

    This is the part of investment that many people forget. They get so fixated on growing their cash that they forget about themselves. Yes, it's important to invest your cash (we'll talk about that in a second), but it's also VITAL to invest in yourself.

By spending some of your profits to level up your skills, it will be beneficial in the long term. To do this, you can invest in your:

- *Education and skills*
  Take short courses, workshops, training programs or webinars to expand your knowledge, improve your public speaking, improve your financial literacy or gain higher certifications. The more you know, the more you grow!

- *Life skills*
  By taking time out to explore new places and connect with more people, you get to experience different things, and grow as a result.

- *Creative pursuits*
  Taking time to indulge your creativity and reading will broaden your mind and talents. If you aim to read every single day, you will grow more than you can ever imagine.

2. **Investing in your BUSINESS.**

   Putting aside a percentage of your profits in your *invest* pot can see you seriously improve your business.

   There will be times when you need to invest back into your business by expanding your product line, improving your business technology, hiring someone to help you, running marketing campaigns or extending into another area. By having cash ready for this, it will alleviate any worries. This will give you the confidence to go for it, leaving your competition in the dust.

3. **Investing your MONEY.**

   If you want to become super wealthy (bring that cha-ching!), then you'll need to start investing now so you can reap the rewards later.

   A popular type of investing is buying stocks.

   Lock, stock and what?

Let me explain… Owning stocks is like owning a small chunk of a company. The way it works is that public companies can raise cash by selling pieces of ownership of the company (called shares) to the public. These are sold on the stock market. When you buy a share of stock in that company (your shares), you become a shareholder and that means you own a little bit of the company. Pretty sweet, hey?

By owning shares, you can reap the rewards when the company does well. You either get a dividend (that's the money it gives to you when it makes a profit) OR it grows the business further and your share price rises higher.

To buy shares you can use online trading platforms such as websites or apps. Another option is using a broker (someone who buys and sells stock for you) to do this. When you want to cash your shares, you can do this through whichever platform, or broker, you are using.

Risky business

It's not all flowers and sunshine, though, as share prices can sometimes go down. Remember, you're in this for the long haul, so don't panic! Normally you'll aim to ride the wave and keep going. Sometimes it takes decades to make money. This kind of investing comes with risk, so do your research, take your time and don't invest more than you can afford to lose. A little can go a long way.

> Imagine you buy stocks in a gaming company called Neon Super Games.
>
> You bought your stock at $15 per share.
>
> And you purchased 20 shares.
>
> $15 x 20 shares = $300.
>
> Now, imagine that after a while the stock value goes up to $23 per share.
>
> This would mean your shares would be worth $460 ($23 x your 20 shares).
>
> That means you have made $160 on those shares (minus any online or broker fees).
>
> Not bad, hey?

Stocks, shares and bears

All these investment terms might seem a little confusing. If your mind is swimming, here's a quick outline to get your head in the game:

- **Bull and bear market**

    A bull market is the term used for stocks going up.

    A bear market is the term used for stocks going down.

    It's easy to remember when you think about the way the animals attack – bulls driving their horns up into the air and bears striking their paws down on their prey.

- **Stock market**

    A virtual marketplace where people buy and sell shares.

- **Public companies**

    This is a company that has gone through the process of offering its shares to the public and is listed on the stock exchange. These companies are often referred to as 'publicly traded' companies. Private companies are NOT listed on stock exchanges.

- **Stock exchange**

    This is a physical place where people trade stock. The New York Stock Exchange (NYSE) is probably one you've heard of. It's the one you see in movies where people in suits are wildly shouting at towering screens with stock prices.

- **Electronic trading platform**

    Most stock trading occurs on electronic trading platforms or exchanges. Major ones include NASDAQ, London Stock Exchange (LSE) and the Australian Securities Exchange (ASX). All of those letters can be quite the mouthful!

- **Dow Jones**

    The Dow Jones Industrial Average is a stock market index that measures the performance of 30 large companies in the US.

- **S&P 500**

    The S&P measures the performance of companies in the US, much like the Dow Jones. But the S&P measures 500 of the largest publicly traded companies.

- **Blue chip stocks**

    These are shares of large, well-established companies with a history of performing consistently. Think of companies like Apple, Coca-Cola or Microsoft.

Now we've covered all the things for you to do with your money, you should be feeling like you have a solid plan and can kick some goals.

Becoming financially savvy is all part of having your own business. And as you've seen, there are a few different ways to make income and grow your money.

Income for doing nothing?

Working on your biz, you'll be making *earned income* (exchanging your time and effort to make money). But long term, you will look at making other kinds of income, such as *investment income* (by owning stocks) or *passive income*, which is income you earn for not actively working.

Hang on. Income for not working? And she waits until this part of the book to tell me about this? *Sign me up!* I hear you say.

Well, it's not income for doing completely nothing. Passive income is a type of income where you get money regularly from something you have set up. So, you have worked really hard on something initially, but once the hard work is done upfront, you don't have to do it again and again.

An example would be building a YouTube channel that generates money from ads or sponsorships. If you can get the channel to attract new people to view it regularly, then this is a winner. Another example would be creating an app. You'd do all the hard work in the beginning developing the app, and then you'd get sales or subscriptions ongoing giving you a smart passive income. Owning rental properties is a classic example of passive income as once you have the property, you earn rent without having to work there each day.

Passive income is a brilliant long-term goal and something you can work towards as you get more business experience.

Quick chapter recap

1. You should set up four money pots: **spend, save, donate and invest.**

2. **Allocate a percentage of your profits** to each of your money pots.

3. Ensure you **spend wisely** (knowing the difference between wants and needs).

4. Set up a bank account to save your money, and **take advantage of interest.**

5. Ensure you **donate your money or time** to a cause.

6. Invest your money, and **invest in yourself!**

CHAPTER 8

Business ideas

If you've read the whole book and still can't think of a business idea, don't panic! It can be tough thinking of ideas to start your own business, but don't worry, I wouldn't leave you high and dry.

Here, I've suggested some biz ideas separated into four categories: techy, craft, outgoing and hands-on from the quiz at the beginning of the book. See if any ideas inspire you!

 Techy

- Computer tutoring business for seniors
- Creating digital products for sale online
- Selling print-on-demand items
- Drone photography service
- Building websites/socials for local businesses
- Online researcher
- Creating social media videos
- Coding
- Live-streaming video games
- Setting up online surveys

 **Crafty**

- Selling baked goods
- Eco-friendly accessories line
- Customised pet-collar business
- Upcycling furniture and selling online
- Selling artwork
- Creating gift baskets
- Making greeting cards
- Designing clothing
- Selling PDF invitations online
- Making bead bracelets

 Outgoing

- YouTube channel
- Children's party entertainer
- Consulting households on eco improvements
- Personal shopper
- Face-painting business
- Local tour guide
- Busking
- Hosting slime parties
- Online yoga teacher
- Podcaster

 **Hands-on**

- Lawn maintenance
- House cleaning
- Car washing
- Dog walking
- Plant-growing service (selling plants and veggies locally)
- Clothes-swap parties
- Pool cleaner
- Swim instructor
- Gift-wrapping service
- Pet grooming

CHAPTER 9

Final message

Entrepreneurship is a long-term journey, and this is just the beginning. Remember, businesses aren't built overnight!

By celebrating your small victories along the way and embracing the challenges, you'll achieve more than you can imagine.

My last piece of advice is to seek out mentors to lean on, learn from and aspire to emulate.

Entrepreneurship is all about your mindset, and the true winners are those who never give up. Keep moving forward, and I promise you'll reach your goals and dreams!

www.ingramcontent.com/pod-product-compliance
Lightning Source LLC
Chambersburg PA
CBHW071126130526
44590CB00056B/2540